The Puzzling Quirks of Regular Expressions

David Mertz, Ph.D.

2021-08-15

Contents

Acknowledgments   **1**

Rights of (Wo)Man   **3**

Credits   **5**

Preface   **7**

Quantifiers and Special Sub-Patterns   **9**
    Wildcard Scope 11
    Words and Sequences 14
    Endpoint Classes 17
    A Configuration Format 19
    The Human Genome 22

Pitfalls and Sand in the Gears   **25**
    Catastrophic Backtracking 26
    Playing Dominoes. 30
    Advanced Dominoes 34
    Sensor Art 38

Creating Functions using Regexen   **41**
    Reimplementing str.count() 43
    Reimplementing str.count() (stricter) 46
    Finding a Name for a Function 51
    Playing Poker (Part 1) 54
    Playing Poker (Part 2) 59
    Playing Poker (Part 3) 63
    Playing Poker (Part 4) 65
    Playing Poker (Part 5) 69

Easy, Difficult, and Impossible Tasks   **73**
   Identifying Equal Counts 75
   Matching Before Duplicate Words 77
   Testing an IPv4 Address 79
   Matching a Numeric Sequence 82
   Matching the Fibonacci Sequence 85
   Matching the Prime Numbers 88
   Matching Relative Prime Numbers 92

Acknowledgments

I thank my friend Miki Tebeka, who invited me to write this book, albeit in slightly different form than the version you see. I am very grateful to my friend Brad Huntting and partner Mary Ann Sushinsky who provided clever ideas in the directions of these puzzles. Thanks to my colleague Lucy Wan, who provided a final proofreading, finding the many silly typos missed on many prior reads.

A number of other friends and family members listened to me enumerate the foibles of another publisher who clings to a cargo-culted toolchain.

With ambivalence, I thank Noam Chomsky for arranging computability into a neat hierarchy, with regular expressions at the bottom.

ACKNOWLEDGMENTS

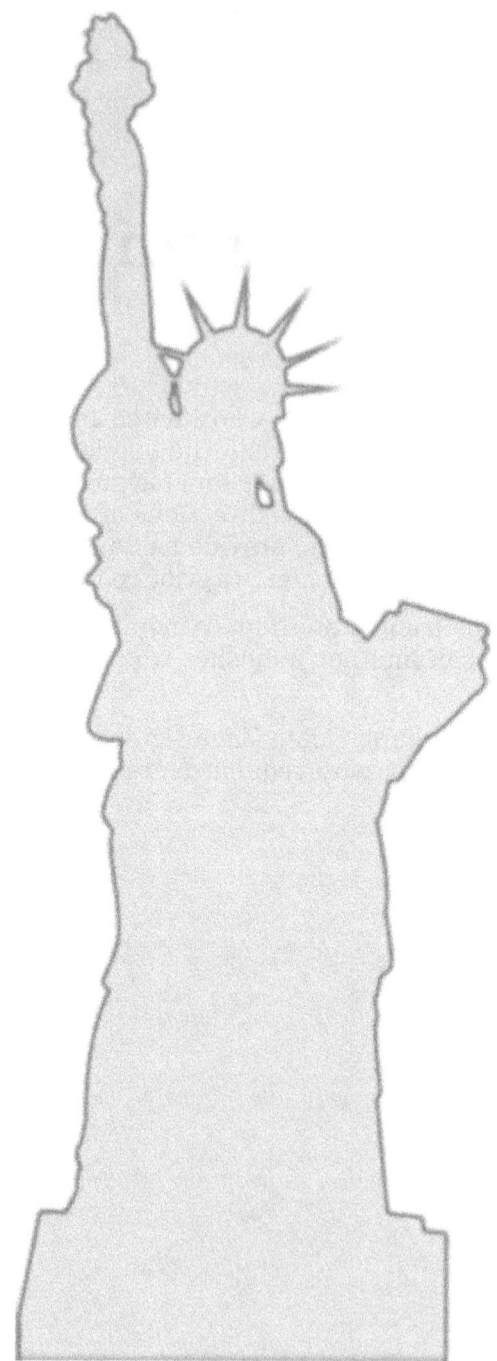

Figure 1: La Liberté éclairant le monde

Rights of (Wo)Man

"Whatever is my right as a man is also the right of another; and it becomes my duty to guarantee as well as to possess."

— Thomas Paine

This book is copyright of David Mertz, 2021.

It is licensed as Creative Commons Attribution-ShareAlike 4.0 (CC BY-SA 4.0). The source is available at:

> https://github.com/DavidMertz/RegEx_Puzzles.

Please feel free to utilize it within these terms (but give me credit).

Figure 2: Striated_Verso

Credits

Cover image: "Alien DNA" by Sven Geier, 2015. Used by permission.

Back cover photo by Mary Ann Sushinsky, 2018. Used by permission.

Images by Jay Trolinger (https://www.spoonflower.com/profiles/ormolu) used by permission: Basket-Verso; Root5spiral-Verso; Striated-Verso; Olives-Verso; Basket-Recto; Naive-Scribble-Verso; Root5spiral-Recto; Naive-Scribble-Recto; Striated-Recto; Olives-Recto

Leo Reynolds (CC BY-NC-SA 2.0): joker-48067975746

Pixabay (https://pixabay.com/service/license/): clown-28772

Dmitry Fomin (CC0 1.0): Atlas_deck_joker_black

freesvg.org (Public Domain): johnny-automatic-right-hand; johnny-automatic-left-hand; johnny-automatic-left-hand; clown-1549219095; Prismatic-DNA-Helix-Circles-3

OpenClipArt (Public Domain): Elegant-Flourish-Frame-Extrapolated-19

Samuel MacGregor Liddel Mathews, "The Goetia: The Lesser Key of Solomon the King" (1904, Public Domain): N_A_B_E_R_I_U_S

Stuck in the Middle with You, by Gerry Rafferty and Joe Egan (Stealer Wheels), 1973:

> Clowns to the left of me! / Jokers to the right! / Here I am stuck in the middle with you.

Figure 3: clown-1549219095

Preface

Regular expressions—sometimes given the playful back formation *regexen* or more neutrally *regex*—are a powerful and compact way of describing patterns in text. Many tutorials and "cheat sheets" exist to understand their syntax and semantics in a formally correct manner. I encourage you to read some of those, if you have not already.

These puzzles begin at a certain point where the formal descriptions leave off. As you work with regexen, you will find subtle pitfalls. A pattern that seems like it should obviously match one thing actually matches something slightly different than you intended. Or perhaps a match pattern has "pathological" behavior and takes far too long. Or sometimes it is simply that a more concise pattern would be clearer in describing what you actually wish to match.

A great many programming languages, libraries, and tools support regular expressions, with relatively minor variations in the syntax used. Such software includes [efr]?grep, sed, awk, *Perl*, *Java*, *.NET*, *JavaScript*, *Julia*, *XML Schema*, or indeed, pretty much every other programming language via a library.

For this book, we will use Python to pose these puzzles. In particular, we will use the standard library module re. Often code samples are used in puzzles and in explanation; where I wish to show the output from code, the example emulates the Python shell with lines starting with >>> (or continuing with ...). Outputs are echoed without a prompt in this case. Where code defines a function that is not necessarily executed in the mention, only the plain code is shown.

While you are reading this book, I strongly encourage you to keep open an interactive Python environment. Many tools enable this, such as the Python REPL (read-evaluate-print-loop) itself, or the IPython enhanced REPL, or Jupyter notebooks, or the IDLE editor that comes with Python, or indeed most modern code editors and IDEs (integrated development environments). A number of online regular expression testers are also available, although those will not capture the the Python calling details. Explanations will follow each puzzle, but trying to work it out in code before reading it is worthwhile. C'mon, not thinking about a puzzle before reading the solution is a cop-out.

Quantifiers and Special Sub-Patterns

Solving the puzzles in this section will require you to have a good understanding of the different quantifiers that regular expressions provide, and to pay careful attention to when you should use subpatterns (themselves likely quantified).

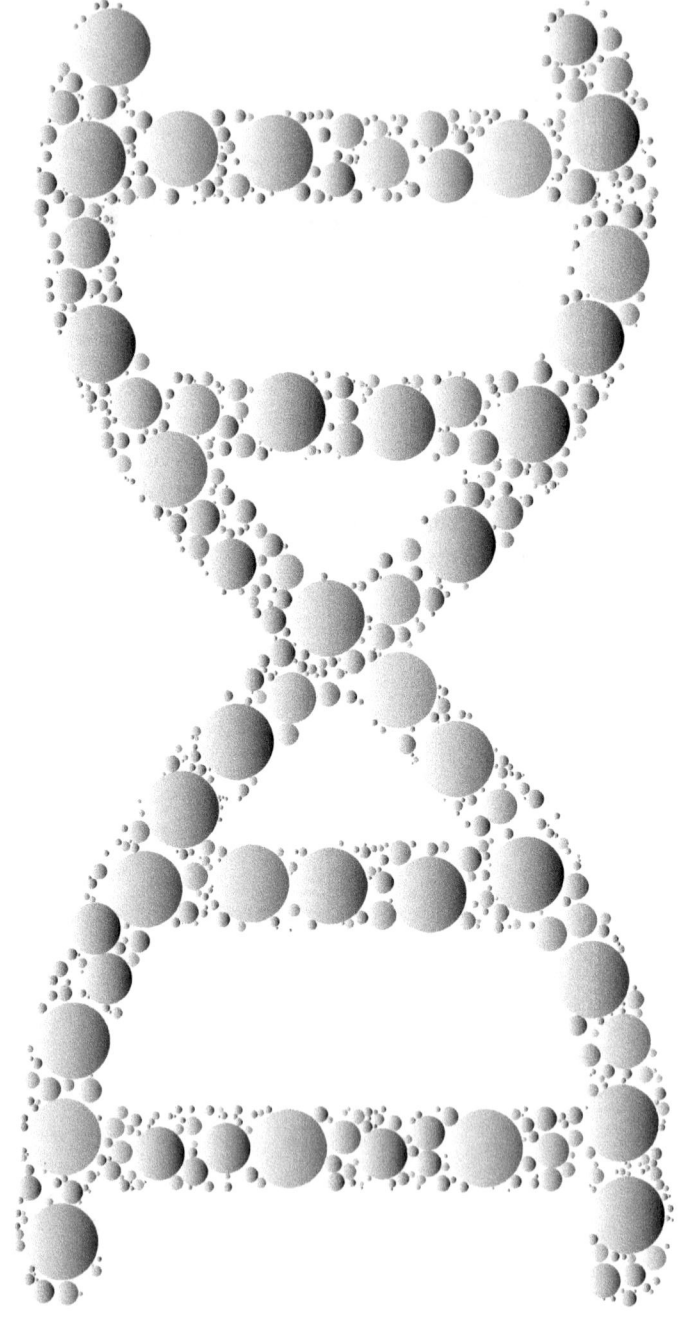

Figure 4: Prismatic-DNA-Helix-Circles-3

Wildcard Scope

A powerful element of Python regular expression syntax—shared by many other regex engines—is the option of creating either "greedy" or "non-greedy" matches. The former matches as much as it possibly can, as long as it finds the later part of a pattern. The latter matches as little as it possibly can to reach the next part of a pattern.

Suppose you have these two regular expressions:

```
pat1 = re.compile(r'x.*y')    # greedy
pat2 = re.compile(r'x.*?y')   # non-greedy
```

And also the following block of text that you want to match. You can think of it as a sort of *lorem ipsum* that only has 'X' words, if you will.

```
txt = """
xenarthral xerically xenomorphically xebec xenomania
xenogenic xenogeny xenophobically xenon xenomenia
xylotomy xenogenies xenografts xeroxing xenons xanthous
xenoglossy xanthopterins xenoglossy xeroxed xenophoby
xenoglossies xanthoxyls xenoglossias xenomorphically
xeroxes xanthopterin xebecs xenodochiums xenodochium
xylopyrography xanthopterines xerochasy xenium xenic
"""
```

You'd like to match all and only words that start with 'X' and end with 'Y'. What pattern makes sense to use, and why? The code to find the words can look like:

```
xy_words = re.findall(_pat, txt)
```

Before you turn the page...

Think about what each pattern will match.

Did this puzzle fool you? Welcome to the world of regular expressions! Both pat1 and pat2 match the wrong thing, but in different ways.

If you liked pat1, you've greedily matched too much. The 'y' might occur in later words (per line), and the match won't end until the last 'y' on a line.

```
>>> for match in re.findall(pat1, txt):
...     print(match)
...
xenarthral xerically xenomorphically
xenogenic xenogeny xenophobically
xylotomy
xenoglossy xanthopterins xenoglossy xeroxed xenophoby
xenoglossies xanthoxyls xenoglossias xenomorphically
xylopyrography xanthopterines xerochasy
```

On each line, the greedy pattern started at the first 'x', which is often not what you want. Moreover, most lines match multiple words, with only the line beginning with 'xylotomy' happening to be the isolated word we actually want. The line that begins with 'xeroxes' is not matched at all, which is what we want.

If you liked pat2 you often get words, but at other times either too much *or too little* might be matched. For example, if 'xy' occurs in a longer word, either as a prefix or in the middle, it can also match.

```
>>> for match in re.findall(pat2, txt):
...     print(match)
...
...
xenarthral xerically
xenomorphically
xenogenic xenogeny
xenophobically
xy
xenoglossy
xanthopterins xenoglossy
xeroxed xenophoby
xenoglossies xanthoxy
xenoglossias xenomorphically
xy
xanthopterines xerochasy
```

By being non-greedy, we stop when the first 'y' is encountered, but as you see, that still is not quite what we want.

What we actually need to focus on for this task is the *word boundaries*. Things that are not lowercase letters cannot be part of matches. In this simple case, non-letters are all spaces and newlines, but other characters might occur in other texts.

We can be greedy to avoid matching prefixes or infixes, but we also want to ignore non-letter characters.

```
>>> pat3 = re.compile(r'x[a-z]*y')
>>> for match in re.findall(pat3, txt):
...     print(match)
...
xerically
xenomorphically
xenogeny
xenophobically
xylotomy
xenoglossy
xenoglossy
xenophoby
xanthoxy
xenomorphically
xylopyrography
xerochasy
```

Everything we matched, anywhere on each line, had an 'x', some other letters (perhaps including 'x's or 'y's along the way), then a 'y'. Whatever came after each match was a non-letter character.

Words and Sequences

In the previous problem, we identified words that started with 'x' and ended with 'y'. You may have noticed, however, that we had already included the assumption that all the words started with 'x'. Perhaps your solution was clever enough not to fall for the danger shown in this puzzle. Namely, perhaps not all words will actually start with 'x' to begin with; i.e. if we try to apply our previous regex to such text.

```
>>> txt = """
expurgatory xylometer xenotime xenomorphically exquisitely
xylology xiphosurans xenophile oxytocin xylogen
xeriscapes xerochasy inexplicably exabyte inexpressibly
extremity xiphophyllous xylographic complexly vexillology
xanthenes xylenol xylol xylenes coextensively
"""
>>> pat3 = re.compile(r'x[a-z]*y')
>>> re.findall(pat3, txt)
['xpurgatory', 'xy', 'xenomorphically', 'xquisitely',
'xylology', 'xy', 'xy', 'xerochasy', 'xplicably', 'xaby',
'xpressibly', 'xtremity', 'xiphophy', 'xy', 'xly',
'xillology', 'xy', 'xy', 'xy', 'xtensively']
```

As you can see, we matched a number of substrings within words, not only whole words. What pattern can you use to actually match only words that start with 'x' and end with 'y'?

Before you turn the page...

Think about what defines word boundaries.

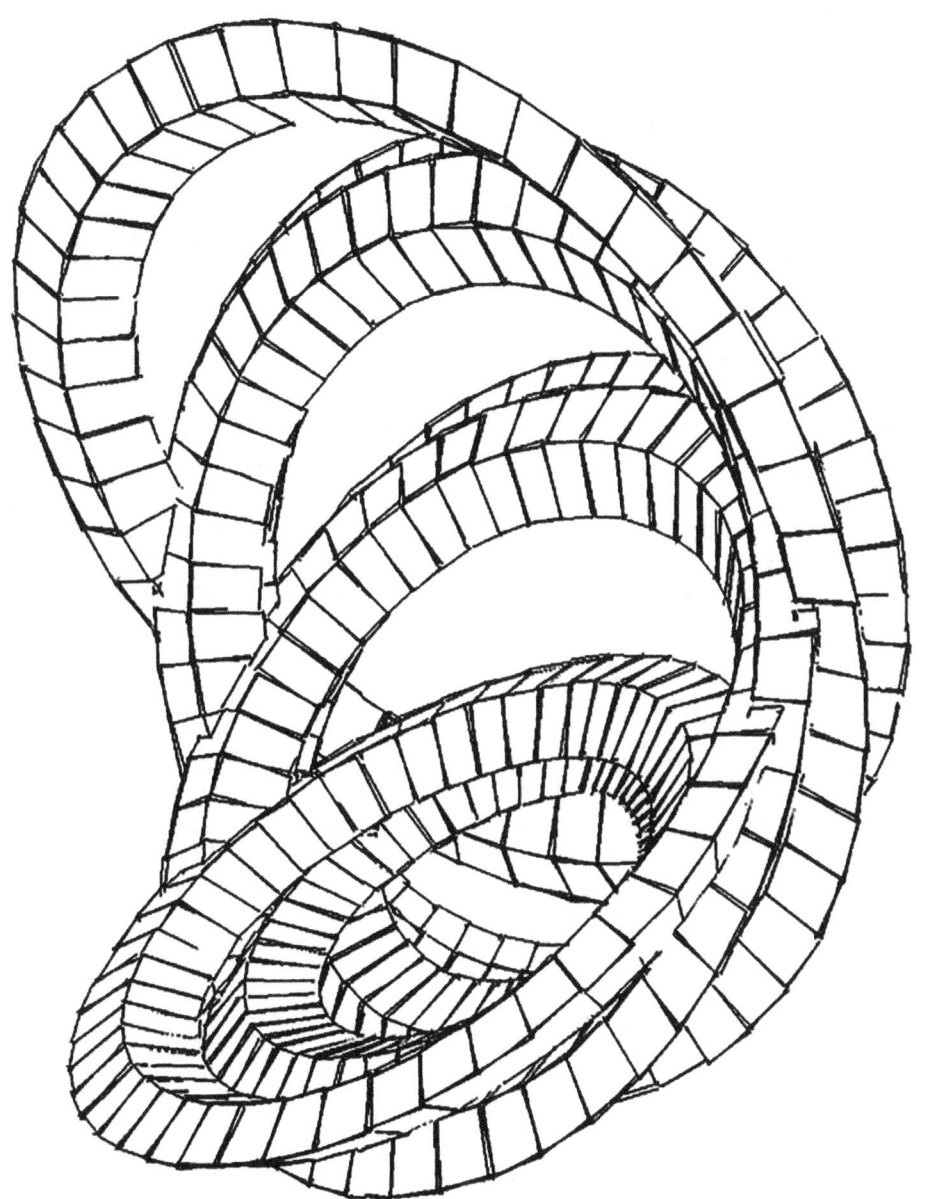

Figure 5: Basket_Recto

There are a few ways you might approach this task. The easiest is to use the explicit "word boundary" special *zero-width match* pattern, spelled as \b in Python and many other regular expression engines.

```
>>> pat4 = re.compile(r'\bx[a-z]*y\b')
>>> re.findall(pat4, txt)
['xenomorphically', 'xylology', 'xerochasy']
```

Less easy ways to accomplish this include using lookahead and lookbehind to find non-matching characters that must "bracket" the actual match. For example:

```
>>> pat5 = r'(?<=^|(?<=[^a-z]))x[a-z]+y(?=$|[^a-z])'
>>> re.findall(pat5, txt)
['xenomorphically', 'xylology', 'xerochasy']
```

One trick here is that when we perform a lookbehind assertion, it must have a fixed width of the match. However, words in our list might either follow spaces or occur at the start of a line. So we need to create an alternation between the zero-width lookbehind and the one non-letter character lookbehind. For the lookahead element, it is enough to say it is *either* end-of-line ($) *or* is a non-letter ([^a-z]).

Endpoint Classes

This puzzle continues the word matching theme of the last two puzzles. However, here we have a new wrinkle. We would like to identify *both* words that start with 'x' and end with 'y', but *also* words that start with 'y' and end with 'x'.

Remembering the word boundary special zero-width pattern we already saw, a first try at this task might be:

```
>>> txt = """
expurgatory xylometer yex xenomorphically exquisitely
xylology xiphosurans xenophile yunx oxytocin xylogen
xeriscapes xerochasy inexplicably yonderly inexpressibly
extremity xerox xylographic complexly vexillology
xanthenes xylenol xylol yexing xylenes coextensively

>>> pat6 = re.compile(r'\b[xy][a-z]*[xy]\b')

>>> re.findall(pat6, txt)
['yex', 'xenomorphically', 'xylology', 'yunx', 'xerochasy',
'yonderly', 'xerox']
"""
```

What went wrong there? Clearly we matched some words we do not want, even though all of them began with 'x' or 'y' and ended with 'x' or 'y'.

Before you turn the page...

Try to refine the regular expression to match what we want.

The first pattern shown allows for either 'x' or 'y' to occur at either the beginning or the end of a word. The word boundaries are handled fine, but this allows words both beginning and ending with 'x', and likewise beginning and ending with 'y'. The character classes at each end of the overall pattern are independent.

This may seem obvious on reflection, but it is very much like errors I myself have made embarrassingly many times in real code. A robust approach is simply to list everything you want as alternatives in a pattern.

```
>>> pat7 = re.compile(r'\b((x[a-z]*y)|(y[a-z]*x))\b')
>>> [m[0] for m in re.findall(pat7, txt)]
['yex', 'xenomorphically', 'xylology', 'yunx', 'xerochasy']
```

In this solution, there is a little bit of Python-specific detail in the function API. The function re.findall() returns tuples when a pattern contains multiple groups. Group 1 will be the whole word, but one or the other of group 2 and 3 will be blank, i.e.:

```
>>> re.findall(pat7, txt)
[('yex', '', 'yex'),
 ('xenomorphically', 'xenomorphically', ''),
 ('xylology', 'xylology', ''),
 ('yunx', '', 'yunx'),
 ('xerochasy', 'xerochasy', '')]
```

A Configuration Format

This exercise requires just a little bit of Python itself, but is mainly about choosing the right regular expression. Let's suppose you have a configuration format that looks like this:

```
config = """
3 = foobar
14=baz
9= fizzbuzz
21=more_stuff,here
"""
```

With a little bit of code, and using a regular expression, you wish to convert text in this format to a dictionary mapping the numbers to the left of the equal sign to the strings to the right. For example, the above example would produce:

```
{3: 'foobar', 14: 'baz', 9: 'fizzbuzz', 21: 'more_stuff,here'}
```

Before you turn the page...

Remember that shapes have edges.

As the example shows, there seems to be flexibility in spaces around the two sides of the equal sign. We should probably assume zero or more spaces are permitted on either side. The format is probably slightly surprising in that we would more commonly use words on the left and numbers on the right in most formats; but it is well-defined enough, and we can stipulate it has a purpose.

The easiest way to capture the relevant information is probably by using groups for each side, which will be exposed by re.findall() and other regular expression functions. We *almost* get the right answer with this:

```
>>> dict(re.findall(r'^(\d+) *= *(.*)$', s, re.MULTILINE))
{'3': 'foobar', '14': 'baz', '9': 'fizzbuzz',
 '21': 'more_stuff,here'}
```

Notice that we required the "multiline" modifier to match on each line of the string. The one problem is that the puzzle requested that numbers appear as numbers, not as strings of digits. There are a number of ways we might achieve that in Python, but one easy one is:

```
>>> {int(k): v for k, v in
            re.findall(r'^(\d+) *= *(.*)$', s, re.MULTILINE)}
{3: 'foobar', 14: 'baz', 9: 'fizzbuzz',
 21: 'more_stuff,here'}
```

Figure 6: Root5spiral_Recto

The Human Genome

Genomics commonly uses a format called FASTA to represent genetic sequences. This puzzle uses a subset of the overall format. Let's provide just a few quick tips. The letters 'A', 'C', 'G', 'T' represent nucleotide bases in DNA. FASTA may also contain the symbol 'N' for "unknown nucleotide" and '-' for "gap of indeterminate length."

As well, in biological organisms, spans of DNA are terminated by "telomeres," which are special sequences indicating that the read mechanism should stop transcription and form a protein. Telomeres are often repeated as much as thousands of times at the ends of sequences. In a gross simplification for this puzzle, let's suppose that three or more repetitions of a telomere indicate the end of a sequence for a protein. In vertebrates, the telomere used is 'TTAGGG'.

In this puzzle, we will ignore the marking of the start of a protein-encoding region, and just assume that all of our strings begin a potential protein encoding.

You would like to create a regular expression that represents a "specific protein encoding" from a (simplified) FASTA fragment. In particular, we need to know exactly which nucleotides are present, and gaps or unknown nucleotides will prevent a match. Moreover, even the telomere repetitions at the end are not permitted (for this puzzle) to have gaps or unknowns.

For this puzzle, assume that all the FASTA symbols are on a single line. Normally as published they have a fixed width less than 80 characters; but newlines are simply ignored. An example of a match:[1]

```
>>> from textwrap import wrap
>>> print('\n'.join(wrap(valid, 60)))
CCCTGAATAATCAAGGTCACAGACCAGTTAGAATGGTTTAGTGTGGAAAGCGGGAAACGA
AAAGCCTCTCTGAATCCTGCGCACCGAGATTCTCCCAAGGCAAGGCGAGGGGCTGTATTG
CAGGGTTCAACTGCAGCGTCGCAACTCAAATGCAGCATTCCTAATGCACACATGACACCC
AAAATATAACAGACATATTACTCATGGAGGGTGAGGGTGAGGGTGAGGGTTAGGGTTAGG
GTTAGGGTTAGGGTTAGGGTTAGGGTTAGGGTTAGGGTTAGGGTTAGGG
```

Using a good pattern, we can identify everything up to, but not including, the telomere repetitions.

---

[1] Some characters shown have Unicode combining diacritics to draw your eye to features. Technically, therefore, some characters shown are not actually the FASTA codes they look similar to.

```
>>> coding = re.search(pat, valid).group()
>>> print('\n'.join(wrap(coding, 60)))
CCCTGAATAATCAAGGTCACAGACCAGTTAGAATGGTTTAGTGTGGAAAGCGGGAAACGA
AAAGCCTCTCTGAATCCTGCGCACCGAGATTCTCCCAAGGCAAGGCGAGGGGCTGTATTG
CAGGGTTCAACTGCAGCGTCGCAACTCAAATGCAGCATTCCTAATGCACACATGACACCC
AAAACTATAACAGACATATTACTCATGGAGGGTGAGGGTGGGGGTGAGGG
```

The next two are failures. The first does not have sufficient repetitions. The second has a non-specific nucleotide symbol:

```
>>> print('\n'.join(wrap(bad_telomere, 60)))
CCCTGAATAATCAAGGTCACAGACCAGTTAGAATGGTTTAGTGTGGAAAGCGGGAAACGA
AAAGCCTCTCTGAATCCTGCGCACCGAGATTCTCCCAAGGCAAGGCGAGGGGCTGTATTG
CAGGGTTCAACTGCAGCGTCGCAACTCAAATGCAGCATTCCTAATGCACACATGACACCC
AAAATATAACAGACATATTACTCATGGAGGGTGAGGGTGAGGGTGAGGGTTAGGGTTAGG
GTTTAGGGTTAGGGTTTAGGGGTTAGGGGTTAGGGATTAGGGTTAGGGTTTAGG

>>> re.search(pat, bad_telomere) or "No Match"
'No Match'

>>> print('\n'.join(wrap(unknown_nucleotide, 60)))
CCCTGAATAATCAAGGTCACAGACCAGTTAGAATGGTTTAGTGTGGAAAGCGGGAAACGA
AAAGCCTCNCTGAATCCTGCGCACCGAGATTCTCCCAAGGCAAGGCGAGGGGCTGTATTG
CAGGGTTCAACTGCAGCGTCGCAACTCAAATGCAGCATTCCTAATGCACACATGACACCC
AAAATATAACAGACATATTACTCATGGAGGGTGAGGGTGAGGGTGAGGGTTAGGGTTAGG
GTTTAGGGTTAGGGTTAGGGGTTAGGGGTTAGGGTTAGGGTTAGGGTTAGGG

>>> re.search(pat, unknown_nucleotide) or "No Match"
'No Match'
```

In the one mismatch, the first several, but not all trailing bases are valid telomeres. In the second mismatch, the 'N' symbol is used. Both of these are valid FASTA encoding, but not the sequences specified for puzzle.

Before you turn the page...

Remember the central dogma of molecular biology.

There are a few key aspects to keep in mind in designing your regular expression. You want to make sure that your pattern begins at the start of the candidate sequence. Otherwise, you could easily match only a valid tail of it.

From there, any sequence of 'C', 'A', 'T', and 'G' symbols is permitted. However, you definitely want to be non-greedy in matching them since no telomeres should be included. The telomere may be repeated any number of times, but at least three. Optionally, repeated telomeres can be required to continue until the end of the candidate sequence, so we must match $ *inside* the lookahead pattern.

pat = r'^([CATG]+?)(?=(TTAGGG){3,}$)'

Pitfalls and Sand in the Gears

As compact and expressive as regular expressions can be, there are times when they simply go disastrously wrong. Be careful to avoid pitfalls, and at least to understand and identify where such difficulties arise.

Catastrophic Backtracking

In this puzzle, we imagine a certain message protocol (as we do in many of the other puzzles). We have n message alphabet that consists of the following symbols:

Codepoint	Name	Appearance
U+25A0	Black Square	■
U+25AA	Black Small Square	▪
U+25CB	White Circle	○
U+25C9	Fisheye	◉
U+25A1	White Square	□
U+25AB	White Small Square	▫
U+25B2	Black Up Triangle	▲
U+25CF	Black Circle	●
U+2404	End Transmition	! (herein)

These geometric characters are attractive and are chosen to avoid thinking of matches in terms of natural language words that some other puzzles utilize. However, feel free in solving it to substitute letters or numerals, which are probably easier to type in your shell. As long as the correspondences are one-to-one, it doesn't matter what symbols are used.

A message in this protocol consists of alternating blocks, belonging to either "type 1" or "type 2." Each block has at least one symbol in it, but type 1 can have any of black square, black up triangle, white circle, fisheye, or white square, in any number and order of each. Type 2 blocks, in contrast, may have white small square, white square, black small square, black circle, or black up triangle, in the same way. Optionally, a space may separate blocks, but it is not required.

The "end of transmission" character indicates the end of a message. An "obvious" pattern to describe a valid message apparently matches appropriately. Some examples are shown below:

Regex: `(^(([■▲○◉□]+) ?([▫□▪●▲]+) ?)+)!`

```
Structure 1/2/1/2   | Message '■▲◉○□▪▫□!' is Valid
Structure 1 2 1 2   | Message '■▲◉ □ ■ ▪□!' is Valid
Missing terminator  | Message '■▲◉○□▪▫□' is Invalid
Structure 1 1 2 1   | Message '▲▲▲ ■◉■ □□● ◉○○!' is Invalid
```

CATASTROPHIC BACKTRACKING

The regex pattern shown actually *is* correct in a mathematical sense. However, it can also become unworkably slow when checking some messages. For example:

```
Quick match     |
                | '■▲○●□□□■●●○□■■●●□▲▲○○●■○■▲▲□□●▲!' is Valid
                | Checked in 0.00 seconds
Quick failure   |
                | '■▲○○■▲□■●●■○■▲▲○○●■□□□□■●●●□■○■!' is Invalid
                | Checked in 0.00 seconds
Failure         | '▲□□▲▲□▲▲▲□□□□□□▲▲□▲□▲□▲X' is Invalid
                | Checked in 4.42 seconds
Slow failure    | '▲□□▲▲▲□▲▲▲□□□□□□□▲▲□▲□▲□▲X' is Invalid
                | Checked in 8.62 seconds
Exponential     | '▲▲▲▲▲▲□□▲▲▲□□□□□□□▲▲□▲□▲□▲▲X' is Invalid
                | Checked in 17.59 seconds
One more symbol | '▲▲▲▲□▲□□▲▲□▲□□□□□□□▲▲□▲□▲□▲▲' is Invalid
                | Checked in 31.53 seconds
```

Why does this happen? Both the valid and the first invalid pattern timed are longer than those that detect mismatches slowly. You can see that the time to determine the last four messages are invalid approximately doubles with each additional character.

Before you look at the explanation, both determine why this occurs and come up with a solution using an alternate regular expression that still validates the message format. Your solution should take a small fraction of a second in all cases (even messages that are thousands of symbols long).

Note that as in other puzzles that use special characters for visual presentation, you may find experimenting easier if you substitute letters or numerals that are easy to type for the symbols used here. It doesn't change the nature of the puzzle at all; it merely might make it easier to use your keyboard.

Before you turn the page...

Try hard to avoid catastrophes.

The reason why the slow-failing messages fail is somewhat obvious to human eyes. None of them end with the "end-of-transmission" character. As you can see, whether they end with an entirely invalid symbol X, or simply with a valid symbol and no terminator, is not significant.

You may want to think about why the quick-failing message also fails. Pause for a moment.

But then notice that the final symbol in that message is "black square" which can only occur in type 1 blocks; in the specification, a type 2 block must always come immediatey before the end-of-transmission terminator. Nonetheless, the regular expression engine figures that out in (significantly) less than 1/100th of a second.

What you need to notice is that the symbol set overlaps between type 1 blocks and type 2 blocks. Therefore, it is ambiguous whether a given symbol belongs to a given block or the next block. If we simply look for a match, *one possible* match is found quickly, when it exists. For example, this message that has only the ambiguous "white square" and "black up triangle" validates immediately:

```
Ambiguous quick  | '▲▲▲▲▢▲▢▢▲▲▢▲▢▢▢▢▢▢▢▲▲▢▲▢▲▢▲▲!' is Valid
                 | Checked in 0.00 seconds
```

However we do not know how many blocks of type 1 and how many of type 2 were created in the match (pedantically, I know enough about the internals of the regular expression engine to know that answer, but we are not guaranteed by the API; it could be different in a later version of the library without breaking compatibility).

Regular expressions are not smart enough to look ahead to the final symbol to make sure it is a terminator, unless we tell it to do so. The produced answer is still *eventually* correct, but it is not as efficient as we would like.

The engine tries every possible permutation of "some symbols in this block, some in that"—which is of exponential complexity on the length of the message—before it finally decides that none match.

Let's solve that by doing a little extra work for the engine. Specifically, before we try to identify alternating type 1 and type 2 blocks, let's just make sure that the entire message is made up of valid symbols that end with the terminator symbol. That check will complete almost instantly, and will eliminate very many (but not all) ways of encountering catastrophic backtracking.

CATASTROPHIC BACKTRACKING

```
Regex: (^(?=^[■▲○◉□■●  ]+!)(([■▲○◉□]+) ?([□□■●▲]+) ?)+)!

Structure 1/2/1/2    | Message '■▲◉□■■□!' is Valid
Structure 1 2 1 2    | Message '■▲◉ □ ■ ■□!' is Valid
Missing terminator   | Message '■▲◉□■■□' is Invalid
Structure 1 1 2 1    | Message '▲▲▲ ■■■ □□□ ○○○!' is Invalid

Quick match          |
       '■▲○◉□□■●◉◉□■■●●□▲▲○○◉■◉■▲▲□◉▲!' is Valid
                     | Checked in 0.00 seconds
Quick failure        |
       '■▲○◉■▲□■●●■◉■▲▲◉◉◉■□□□□■●●●□■◉■!' is Invalid
                     | Checked in 0.00 seconds
Failure              | '▲□□▲▲□▲▲▲□□□□□□▲▲□▲□▲□▲X' is Invalid
                     | Checked in 0.00 seconds
Slow failure         | '▲□□▲▲▲□▲▲▲□□□□□□□▲▲□▲□▲□▲X' is Invalid
                     | Checked in 0.00 seconds
Exponential          | '▲▲▲▲▲▲□□▲▲▲□□□□□□□▲▲□▲□▲□▲▲X' is Invalid
                     | Checked in 0.00 seconds
One more symbol      | '▲▲▲▲□▲□□▲▲□▲□□□□□□□▲▲□▲□▲□▲▲' is Invalid
                     | Checked in 0.00 seconds
Ambiguous quick      | '▲▲▲▲□▲□□▲▲□▲□□□□□□□▲▲□▲□▲□▲▲!' is Valid
                     | Checked in 0.00 seconds
```

Playing Dominoes

Dominoes is an old family of games dating at least from the Yuan Dynasty (around 1300 CE). The game is played with tiles on which each half of one side is marked, generally with a number of dots corresponding to a number. Specific games vary in their rules, but most require matching the symbol or number on half of a tile with the corresponding symbol on another tile.

There are, in fact, Unicode characters for all the domino tiles that have zero to six dots on each half. We will come back to those characters in the next puzzle. As a reminder, some of those Unicode characters are listed in this table.

U-1F03B   Domino Tile Horizontal-01-03

U-1F049   Domino Tile Horizontal-03-03

U-1F04C   Domino Tile Horizontal-03-06

U-1F05C   Domino Tile Horizontal-01-03

The actual codepoints are hard to enter, and hard to see unless they are displayed at a large font size (as here). But to illustrate the "game" our regex will play, we can show examples of, first, a valid/winning pattern:

And second, an invalid/losing pattern:

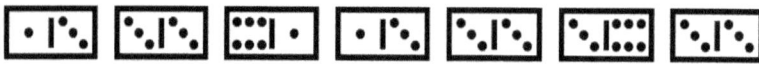

PLAYING DOMINOES

In this game, tiles are placed in linear order, and two may occur adjacently only if they have the same number of dots where they "touch." Unlike with physical tiles, these symbols may not be turned around, but maintain the same left-right order.

Because of the display and entry problems mentioned, we play an alternative version of this game in which "tiles" are spelled as ASCII characters. For example, the winning and losing patterns shown as Unicode characters are as follows in their ASCII versions:

Winning
{1:3}{3:3}{3:6}{6:1}{1:3}{3:3}{3:3}

Losing
{1:3}{3:3}{6:1}{1:3}{3:3}{3:6}{3:3}

Plays may be of any length. Infinitely many tiles, with ends having the numbers 1-6 in every combination, are available. Write a regular expression that distinguishes every winning play from a losing play. Note that any character sequence that doesn't define a series of one or more tiles is trivially losing.

Before you turn the page...

You might do this more efficiently than your first thought.

Because of our ASCII encoding we have a shortcut available for the regular expression that can judge whether a play is winning. This would not be available with the icon characters for the domino tiles.

The same digit must occur at the end of one tile, and again at the start of the next tile. Therefore, we can shortcut specifically matching '3's with '3's and '5's with '5's. Instead, we can just use a lookahead to match a backreference group.

```
# Mismatched ends in bad, malformed syntax in awful
>>> good  =   '{1:3}{3:3}{3:6}{6:1}{1:3}{3:3}{3:3}'
>>> bad   =   '{1:3}{3:3}{6:1}{1:3}{3:3}{3:6}{3:3}'
>>> awful =   '{1:3}{{3:5}}{5:2}'

>>> pat = r'^(({[1-6]:([1-6])})(?=$|{\3))+$'

>>> for play in (good, bad, awful):
...     match = re.search(pat, play)
...     if match:
...         print(match.group(), "wins!")
...     else:
...         print(play, "loses!")
...
{1:3}{3:3}{3:6}{6:1}{1:3}{3:3}{3:3} wins!
{1:3}{3:3}{6:1}{1:3}{3:3}{3:6}{3:3} loses!
{1:3}{{3:5}}{5:2} loses!
```

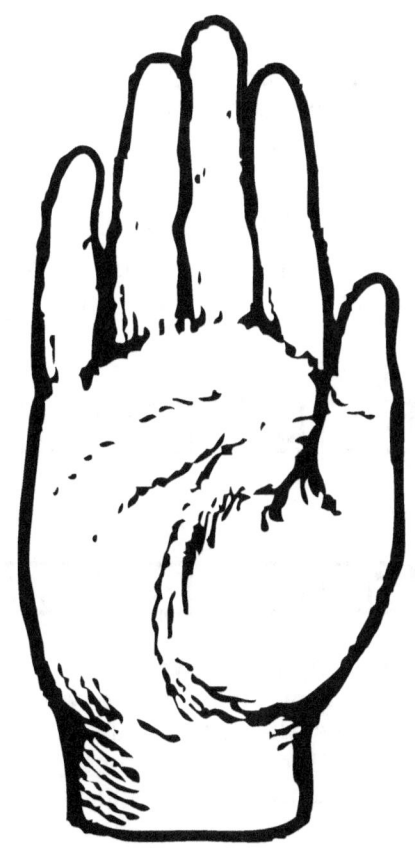

Figure 7: johnny-automatic-right-hand

Advanced Dominoes

As the last puzzle showed, there are Unicode characters for domino tiles. In the last puzzle, we played a game of evaluating whether a particular sequence of "tiles"—represented by ASCII sequences— was winning plays. However, in that last puzzle, we took a shortcut by taking advantage of the internal structure of the ASCII representation.

It is not too hard to match domino tiles as their Unicode characters. For example, this pattern matches any linear sequence of (horizontal) tiles:

```
pat = (r'[\N{Domino Tile Horizontal-00-00}-'
       '\N{Domino Tile Horizontal-06-06}]+)'
```

Most of those sequences will not be winning plays, of course. Recall the examples of winning and losing plays from the prior lesson:

Winning:

Losing:

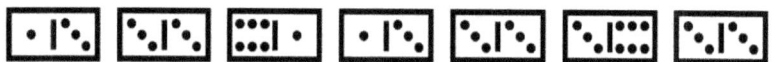

For this game we will simplify in two ways. First, rather than use hard-to-enter and hard-to-see tile icons, we will use ASCII characters. In fact, if we only want the tiles with numbers from 1-6 on their ends, that gives us exactly 36 of them. Conveniently, that happens to be the same number of symbols as there are numerals plus capital letters (in English).

However, this puzzle is simplified further by only utilizing four of the 36 possible tiles. Each of those is given the following ASCII representation. The letters are not mnemonic, but at least they are easy to type.

ADVANCED DOMINOES

Codepoint	Name	Substitute
U+1F03B	Domino Tile Horizontal-01-03	A
U+1F049	Domino Tile Horizontal-03-03	B
U+1F04C	Domino Tile Horizontal-03-06	C
U+1F05C	Domino Tile Horizontal-06-01	D

Repeating our winning and losing examples with this encoding:

```
win  = 'ABCDABB'
lose = 'ABDABCB'
```

Plays may be of any length, and you have infinitely many of each of the four tile types to use. Write a regular expression that distinguishes every winning play from a losing play. Note that any character outside the tile symbol set is trivially losing.

Before you turn the page...

Thoughts about digrams are always pleasant thoughts.

Figure 8: Root5spiral_Verso

ADVANCED DOMINOES

It probably comes as no surprise to you that a larger tile set would require a larger regular expression to match winning plays. But the principle would remain the same if you used more tiles, up to all of them.

The basic idea here is that you want each tile to be followed by a tile from some subset of other tiles. Namely, those that begin with the same number of dots that the current tile ends with.

Of course, a given tile might be the end of a play, so you have to include that option in your lookahead pattern. You also definitely want a match to begin at the start of the play and end at the end of the play, so be sure to include the match patterns ^ and $ to indicate that.

```
>>> win = 'ABCDABB'
>>> lose = 'ABDABCB'
>>> pat = r'^(A(?=$|[BC])|B(?=$|[BC])|C(?=$|D)|D(?=$|A))+$'
>>> re.search(pat, win)
<re.Match object; span=(0, 7), match='ABCDABB'>
>>> re.search(pat, lose) or "No Match"
'No Match'
```

Sensor Art

A hypothetical data format uses a character string to represent state transitions in a two-state system. For example, this might be the status of some sort of electrical sensor. Each string represents a "signal" of some time duration.

The signal can occupy the "high" state for any duration, and it can occupy the "low" state for any duration. Moreover, the transition between the two can either be "fast" or "slow," but it must stay in a state for at least one time interval after each transition.

The format has a mnemonic version that uses simple ASCII art to represent states and transitions. However, it also has a letter-based version you may wish to play with instead, simply because many of the line drawing characters have special meanings in regex syntax. Special characters can be escaped, but it makes the patterns harder to read.

Some valid and invalid signals are below:

```
valid_1a   = "_/^^^\_/^|___|^\____|^^\__/"
valid_1b   = "LuHHHdLuHFLLLFHdLLLLFHHdLLu"
valid_2a   = "____/^^^^^^"
valid_2b   = "LLLLuHHHHHH"

invalid_1a = "_^/^^^/__\_"
invalid_1b = "LHuHHHuLLdL"
invalid_2a = "|\/|"
invalid_2b = "FduF"
invalid_3a = "__/^^|__X__/"
invalid_3b = "LLuHHFLLXLLu"
invalid_4a = "|_^|__"
invalid_4b = "FLHFLL"
```

Signals valid_1a and valid_1b represent the same measurement. In the correspondence, L maps to _ (low state), u maps to / (up transition), d maps to \ (down transition), H maps to ^ (high state), and F maps to | (fast transition). Likewise, valid_2a and valid_2b are equivalent and simpler signals with just one up transition, but a duration in each state.

The invalid signals similarly have the different character options. Signals invalid_1a or invalid_1b have *several* problems. Low and high states are adjacent with no transition (not permitted). An alleged up transition occurs from the high state (also not permitted). Moreover, a down transition occurs from the low state. The chief problem with invalid_2a or invalid_2b are that they have transitions with no states in between, which is also prohibited. In the case of invalid_3a or invalid_3b, the states and transitions are generally fine, but there is an invalid symbol thrown in.

You wish to define a regular expression that will match *all* and *only* valid signal strings. Pick which character set you wish to define—"ASCII" or "linedraw," but not intermixed—and find the pattern you need.

That is, find the pattern that will work *only if* regular expressions are sufficiently powerful to perform this test.

Before you turn the page...

Find a matching pattern, if possible.

This puzzle *is* solvable with regexen. There are a few observations to keep in mind when thinking about it. The rules for a valid signal actually consist of just two constraints:
- All signals must be drawn only from the limited alphabet
- Only a subset of *digrams* of symbols are valid

In particular, since the alphabet is 5 symbols, there are 25 possible digrams. However, only 10 of those can occur in a valid signal. You might be tempted simply to match any number of repetitions of valid digrams. However, that would go wrong in examples like `invalid_4`. Symbols 1 and 2 might form a valid digram, and symbols 3 and 4 might also be a valid digram; but quite possibly symbols 2 and 3 are not a valid digram together.

What we need to do is *lookahead* to two symbols, but then only match one symbol. Moreover, we need to consider the special case where the regex engine is currently looking at the final symbol in the signal, since that needs to be included as well. So an alternate lookahead of "anything then end" is used. Notice that we can use the '.' wildcard because the digram was already guaranteed by the *prior* lookahead in the repetition.

Shown first is `patB` which matches the ASCII version of the format, then the much more difficult to read `patA` which uses several symbols requiring escaping for the pattern definition since they would otherwise have regex meanings.

```
patB  =   (r'^(((?=LL|Lu|LF|HH|Hd|HF|uH|dL|FH|FL)'
           r'|(?=.$))[LHudF])+$')

patA  =   (r'^(((?=__|_/|_\||\^\^|\^\\|\^\||/\^|\\_|\||\^|\|_)'
           r'|(?=.$))[_\^/\\|])+$')
```

Creating Functions using Regexen

Very often in Python, or in other programming languages, you will want to wrap a regular expression in a small function rather than repeat it inline.

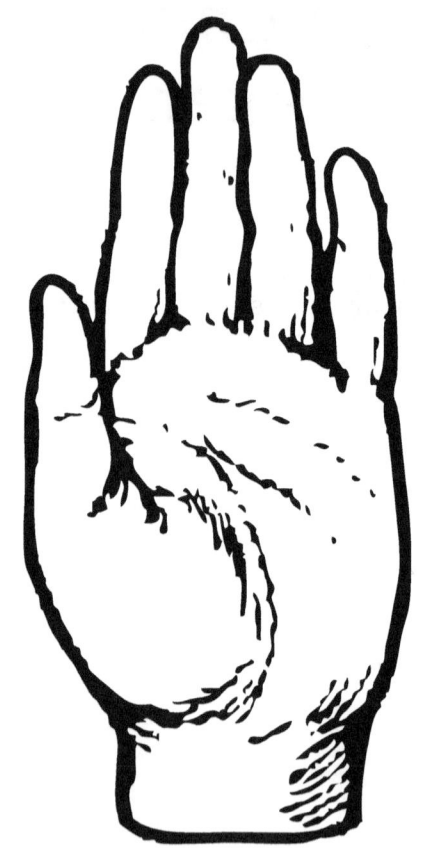

Figure 9: johnny-automatic-left-hand

Reimplementing str.count()

The Python method `str.count()` is widely useful to find substrings inside a larger string. For example, here is some typical code you might write:

```
# Lyric from song "Hot Knife" by Fiona Apple
>>> s = """If I'm butter, if I'm butter
If I'm butter, then he's a hot knife
He makes my heart a CinemaScope screen
Showing the dancing bird of paradise
"""
>>> s.count('e')
15
>>> s.count('tt')
3
```

Imagine that Python did not have the method `str.count()` but you wished to implement a similar function by utilizing regular expressions, with the signature:

```
def my_count(substring: str, string: str) -> int:
    # re.sub(..., ...)   # maybe something like this?
    ...
```

Before you turn the page...

How can a regex count the substring occurrences?

Two functions in the Python re module seem especially likely to be useful. The re.sub() function will replace a pattern with something else. We might try a solution using that, for example:

```
>>> def my_count(substring, string):
...     return len(re.sub(fr"[^{substring}]", "", string))
>>> my_count('e', s)
15
>>> my_count('tt', s)     # Oops, this goes wrong
10
```

So that try is not quite correct. It will count single characters fine, but for larger substrings it gets confused. In the example, the inversion of the character class is [^tt] which is the same as simply being *not a "t"*. In other words, we counted the "t"'s not the "tt"'s. Even if the substring hadn't been the same letter twice, we would count the individual letters in the pattern.

We can fix this with a more complex regular expression (think about how as a bonus puzzle), but even easier is using re.findall():

```
>>> def my_count(substring, string):
...     return len(re.findall(fr"{substring}", string))
>>> my_count('e', s)
15
>>> my_count('tt', s)
3
```

Figure 10: Striated_Recto

Reimplementing str.count() (stricter)

In the last puzzle, we reimplemented `str.count()` using regular expressions. However, the solutions I presented—and most likely the solution you arrvied at on your own—ultimately came down to utilizing `len()` on something derived from the original string (to count the number of matches found).

For this puzzle, pretend that Python also does not have the `len()` function; and also do not implement your own equivalent by, for example, looping through an iterable and incrementing a counter when a substring is found. One way to express this is that your function should use no numeric variables or values.

In fact, what we want as the result is a string that represents the number of the count, not an actual number. To simplify the problem, however, we can assume that we are only counting single characters, not substrings in general. In fact, to simplify even more, let's just assume the input strings are exclusively nucleotide symbols like in the example below (generalizing this isn't too difficult). A solution will look something like this:

```
>>> def let_count(char: str, string: str) -> str:
...     # maybe a while loop, some calls to re.something()
...
```

For example, using it to count nucleotides:

```
>>> mRNA = '''
GGGAAATAAGAGAGAAAAGAAGAGTAAGAAGAAATATAAGACCCCGGCGCCGCCACCAT
GTTCGTGTTCCTGGTGCTGCTGCCCCTGGTGAGCAGCCAGTGCGTGAACCTGACCACCC
GGACCCAGCTGCCACCAGCCTACACCAACAGCTTCACCCGGGGCGTCTACTACCCCGAC
AAGGTGTTCCGGAGCAGCGTCCTGCACAGCACCCAGGACCTGTTCCTGCCCTTCTTCAG
CAACGTGACCTGGTTCCACGCCATCCACGTGAGCGGCACCAACGGCACCAAGCGGTTCG
ACAACCCCGTGCTGCCCTTCAACGACGGCGTGTACTTCGCCAGCACCGAGAAGAGCAAC
ATCATCCGGGGCTGGATCTTCGGCACCACCCTGGACAGCAAGACCCAGAGCCTGCTGAT
CGTGAATAACGCCACCAACGTGGTGATCAAGGTGTGCGAGTT
'''
```

REIMPLEMENTING STR.COUNT() (STRICTER)

```
>>> let_count('G', mRNA)
'120'
>>> let_count('C', mRNA)
'152'
>>> let_count('T', mRNA)
'74'
>>> let_count('A', mRNA)
'109'
```

Before you turn the page...

Write a Python function with the restrictions given.

CREATING FUNCTIONS USING REGEXEN

This one turns out to be somewhat difficult, but also to be *possible*, which is itself sort of amazing. No numbers whatsoever are involved in the solution shown. No counters, no integer variables, no Python functions returning numbers.

We also do not need to use any Python string methods, although it is fair to note that some of what is performed via regular expressions might be more simple to express as string methods. The function can perform strictly and only regular expression operations... along with a little bit of Python looping (but never over numbers).

We use two sentinels in alternation for the loop, indicating either the number of items at a certain power of ten, or the number at the next higher power. A dictionary can map zero to nine repetitions of a sentinel to the corresponding numeral, but leave the rest of the string unchanged.

```
# Group 1: zero or more leading @'s
# Group 2: some specific number of _'s
# Group 3: anything until end; digits expected
counter = {
    r'(^@*)(_____)(.*$)': r'\g<1>9\g<3>',
    r'(^@*)(_____)(.*$)': r'\g<1>8\g<3>',
    r'(^@*)(_____)(.*$)': r'\g<1>7\g<3>',
    r'(^@*)(_____)(.*$)': r'\g<1>6\g<3>',
    r'(^@*)(_____)(.*$)': r'\g<1>5\g<3>',
    r'(^@*)(____)(.*$)': r'\g<1>4\g<3>',
    r'(^@*)(___)(.*$)': r'\g<1>3\g<3>',
    r'(^@*)(__)(.*$)': r'\g<1>2\g<3>',
    r'(^@*)(_)(.*$)': r'\g<1>1\g<3>',
    r'(^@*)(_*)(.*$)': r'\g<1>0\g<3>'
}
```

A first step is to map the target character to a sentinel. It would be easy to extend the main function to map a generic regular expression pattern to that same sentinel.

The two sentinels underscore and at-sign are used here, but some rare Unicode codepoint in the astral plane—or even a private-use codepoint—could just as well be used instead if collision with the initial string were a concern.

```
def let_count(c, s):
    # First lines only convert single char to sentinel,
    # but could be generalized to any regex pattern
    # Remove everything that isn't the target character
    s = re.sub(fr'[^{c}]', '', s)
    # Convert the target to the underscore sentinel
    s = re.sub(fr'{c}', '_', s)

    # Loop indefinitely: do not know number digits needed
    while True:
        # Ten underscores become an @ sign
        s = re.sub(r'_____', '@', s)
        for k, v in counter.items():
            # Replace trailing underscores with a digit
            new = re.sub(k, v, s)
            # Some pattern matched, so exit the loop
            if new != s:
                s = new
                break
        # If we have only digits, we are done
        if re.match(r'^[0-9]*$', s):
            return s
        # Convert from "unprocessed" to "todo" sentinels
        s = re.sub('@', '_', s)
```

Figure 11: Olives_Verso

Finding a Name for a Function

Suppose you come across some code that a previous employee on your project, long moved on and unavailable, wrote. Their code passes unit tests and integration tests, so it probably does the right thing. But they have not given a useful name or documentation for a certain function:

```
def is_something(s):
    return not re.match(r'^(.+?)\1+$', s)
```

For this puzzle, simply provide a good name and a docstring for this function, to be kind to later programmers.

Before you turn the page...

Code is read far more often than it is written.

This puzzle certainly has many possible answers. For all of them, understanding what the regular expression is doing is the crucial element. The short pattern might look odd, and you need to figure it out. Here is a possibility.

```
def repeated_prefix(s):
    """Look for any prefix string in 's' and match only if
    that prefix is repeated at least once, but it might be
    repeated many times.  No other substring may occur
    between the start and end of the string for a match.
    """
    return not re.match(r'^(.+?)\1+$', s)
```

Figure 12: Atlas_deck_joker_black

Playing Poker (Part 1)

In earlier puzzles, we had fun playing dominoes. For the next few puzzles, let's play poker. In particular, let's say that a player has five cards, and we wish to compare two hands to each other. We will do this, over several puzzles, by building up small functions to answer various questions.

As much as possible, you should use regular expressions to express the logic; however, a few of the questions will require a little bit of non-regex code as well. First, let's remind ourselves of the ranking of different hands of 5 cards. Our encoding will simplify card representations a little bit. Specifically, the card that might be called, e.g., 10♥ will be called T♥ so that every card is a two symbol combination.

- Straight flush, e.g. J♣ T♣ 9♣ 8♣ 7♣
- Four of a kind, e.g. A♥ 3♠ 3♥ 3♦ 3♣
- Full house, e.g. K♠ K♣ 6♥ 6♦ 6♣
- Flush, e.g. J♦ 9♦ 6♦ 5♦ 2♦
- Straight, e.g. 9♦ 8♣ 7♣ 6♥ 5♣
- Three of a kind, e.g. Q♣ 8♠ 8♦ 8♣ 3♥
- Two pairs, e.g. J♠ J♣ 9♥ 8♥ 8♦
- One pair, e.g. A♥ K♦ 4♠ 4♥ 3♠
- High card, e.g. K♠ 9♥ 8♣ 4♥ 2♣

Within the same kind of hand, other rules come into play. Let's ignore those for now. We'd like two support functions to start. First, you should write a function `prettify(hand)` that takes an easier-to-type representation of suits as 'S', 'H', 'D', 'C', and turns the hands into their Unicode symbols.

PLAYING POKER (PART 1)

The second and more difficult function for this puzzle asks you to make sure all the cards are sorted in descending order (as in the examples), where aces are always considered high, and the suits are ordered spades, hearts, diamonds, clubs.

This second function, cardsort(hand), uses more Python than regular expressions per se, so just read the solution if you are less comfortable with Python itself.

Before you turn the page...

Functions are a big help in larger programs.

The truth is, we do not genuinely *need* regular expressions for either of these support functions. But we do have the opportunity to use them. First let's transform any ASCII version of a hand into the Unicode version. Along the way, we make sure the hand consists of five valid ASCII cards.

```
def prettify(hand):
    assert re.search(r'^([2-9TJQKA][SHDC] ?){5}$', hand)
    symbols = {'S': '\u2660', 'H': '\u2665',
               'D': '\u2666', 'C': '\u2663'}
    for let, suit in symbols.items():
        hand = re.sub(let, suit, hand)
    return hand
```

Sorting uses mostly plain Python techniques. In particular, we can rely on the fact that Python's sort is *stable*. This means the order will not change between equivalent elements. Therefore, sorting first by suit, then by number will be guaranteed to have the right overall effect.

```
def cardsort(hand):
    def by_num(card):
        map = {'T':'A', 'J':'B', 'Q':'C',
               'K':'D', 'A':'E'}
        num = card[0]
        return num if num not in 'AKQJT' else map[num]

    def by_suit(card):
        map = {'\u2663': 1, '\u2666': 2,
               '\u2665': 3, '\u2660': 4}
        return map[card[1]]

    hand = re.split(' ', hand)
    hand.sort(key=by_suit, reverse=True)
    hand.sort(key=by_num, reverse=True)
    return ' '.join(hand)
```

PLAYING POKER (PART 1)

Combining these:

```
>>> cardsort(prettify('8C AS 4H KS 2C'))
'A♠ K♠ 8♣ 4♥ 2♣'
```

We will need more regular expressions in the next few puzzles which continue this poker theme.

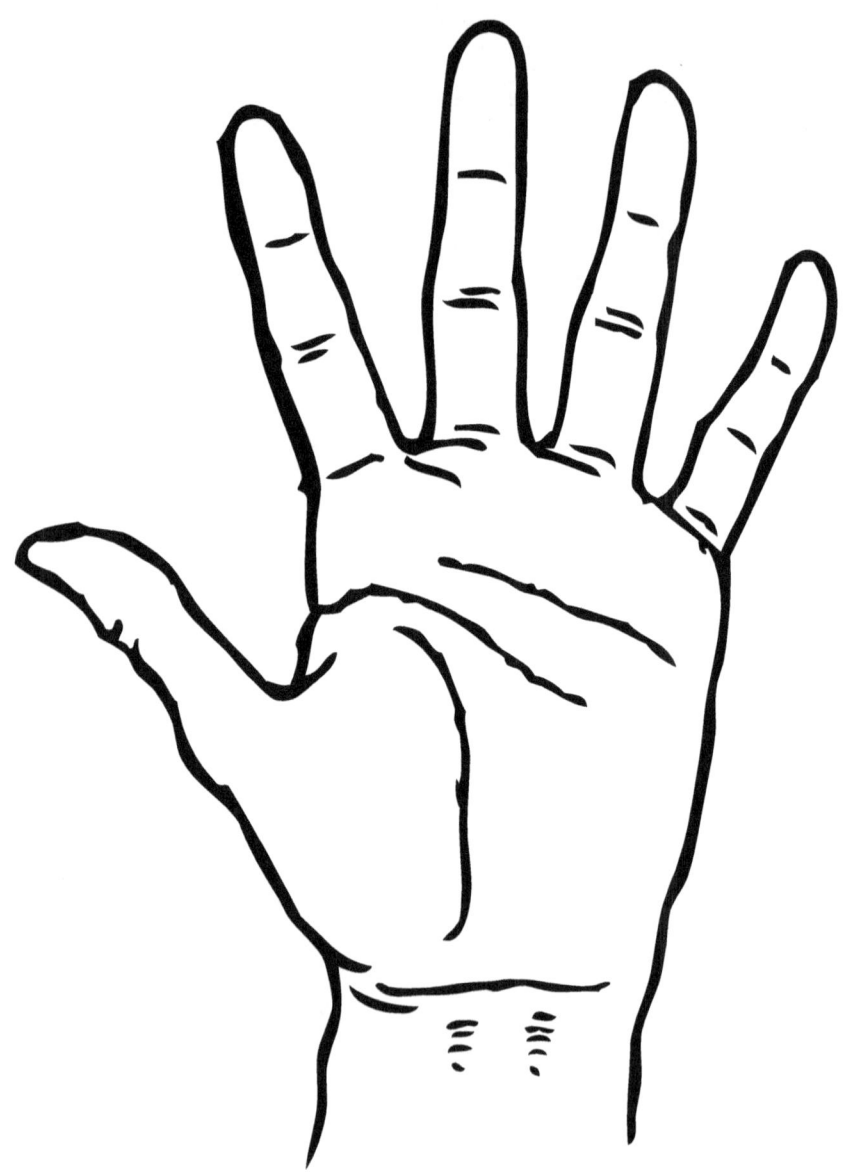

Figure 13: johnny-automatic-left-hand-spread

Playing Poker (Part 2)

In the last puzzle, you converted "poker hands" from ASCII to Unicode suit symbols, and you also made sure that hands are listed in canonical descending card order.

For this puzzle, you want to start using regular expressions to figure out whether hands belong to various kinds. Here's an obvious trick we can use as a shortcut:

```
def is_straight_flush(hand):
    return is_straight(hand) and is_flush(hand)
```

For this puzzle, you wish to write the functions is_flush(hand) and is_straight(hand), continuing with the assumption that hands are represented in the same manner as the last puzzle (including the cards being in descending order). Feel free to use the prettify() function you wrote if it makes entering test cases easier.

Before you turn the page...

Large buildings are built from small bricks.

Identifying a flush is somewhat easier. Moreover, if we are clever, we can add two features to the function not specifically required in the puzzle. We can make it work identically with the ASCII codes like 'S' for spaces and 'H' for hearts simultaneously with the Unicode special symbols.

But while we are creating the function, we can also return extra "truthy" information in the return value. Namely, if it *is* a flush, let's return the suit also.

```
>>> def is_flush(hand):
...     match = re.search(r'^.(.)(.*\1){4}$', hand)
...     return match.group(1) if match else False

>>> is_flush('J♣ T♣ 9♣ 8♣ 7♣')
'♣'
>>> is_flush('J♦ 9♦ 6♦ 5♦ 2♦')
'♦'
>>> is_flush('J♦ 9♥ 6♦ 5♦ 2♦')
False
>>> is_flush('JD 9H 6D 5D 2D')
False
>>> is_flush('JD 9D 6D 5D 2D')
'D'
```

For checking for straights, let's add a similar bit of extra information in the return value. Obviously, if the hand is not a straight, we should return False. But if it is one, we can return the high card number for later use. Those are all "truthy" values (like all strings).

```
>>> def is_straight(hand):
...     pat = r'[ SHDC\u2660\u2665\u2666\u2663]'
...     h = re.sub(pat, '', hand)
...     match = re.search(h, 'AKQJT98765432')
...     return h[0] if match else False
```

As with the first function, we might as well be friendly in accepting the ASCII version of suits, even though they could always be improved with prettify() if necessary. The pattern looks for everything that is a suit character or a space, and strips it out to create a simplified "hand."

PLAYING POKER (PART 2)

With the simplified hand of just "numbers," we know that any straight must be a substring of the run of all numbers. We do not check again that the length is 5, trusting that other functions have validated this. We could easily add that if we wanted, of course.

At this point, you might consider a richer implementation of is_straight_flush(). Perhaps this:

```
>>> def is_straight_flush(hand):
...     s = is_straight(hand)
...     f = is_flush(hand)
...     return s+f if s and f else False

>>> is_straight_flush('JD TD 9D 8D 7D')
'JD'
>>> is_straight_flush('JD TD 9H 8D 7D')
False
```

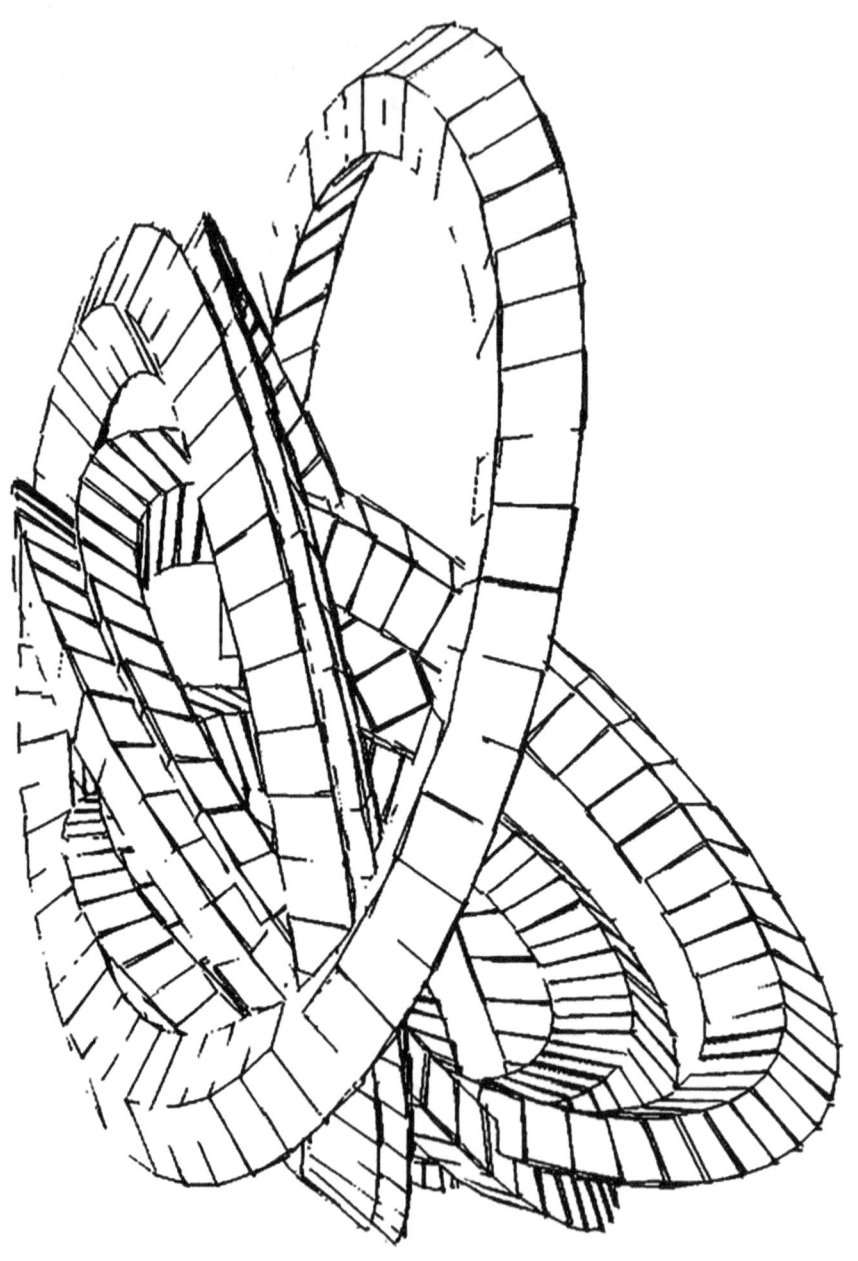

Figure 14: Basket_Verso

Playing Poker (Part 3)

In this puzzle let's continue with matching poker hands. We handled straights and flushes in the last puzzle (and straight flushes by obvious combination). There are some other types of hands to consider now.

The next several types of hand have containing relationships among them. That is, just like a straight flush is both a straight and a flush, four-of-a-kind is trivially also three-of-a-kind and a pair. A full house is both three-of-a-kind and a pair. However, for our purposes, we will simply assume the various tests are performed in appropriate descending order of strength. The first successful test will be the classified type of the hand.

For the next few puzzles, therefore, write these functions:

- is_four_of_kind(hand)
- is_full_house(hand)
- is_three_of_kind(hand)
- is_two_pairs(hand)
- is_pair()

This and the next few puzzles cover the various functions. See if you can solve all of them (possibly using shared functionality) before looking at the discussion.

Before you turn the page...

You better cheat, cheat, if you can't win.

If we have a four-of-a-kind, then the kind must occur in either the first or second card. In fact, if we retain our assumption that the cards are completely ordered, then the four can only occur as the initial four or the final four. But the following implementation does not rely on that ordering:

```
>>> def is_four_of_kind(hand):
...     hand = re.sub(r'[^AKQJT98765432]', '', hand)
...     pat = r'^.?(.)(.*\1){3}'
...     match = re.search(pat, hand)
...     # Return the card number as truthy value
...     return match.group(1) if match else False
...
>>> is_four_of_kind('6H 6D 6S 6C 3S')  # sorted
'6'
>>> is_four_of_kind('6♦ 3♠ 6♥ 6♠ 6♣')  # not sorted
'6'
>>> is_four_of_kind('6H 6D 6S 4C 3S')  # not four-of-kind
False
```

The first step is to remove everything that isn't a card number. Then we either match nothing or the first character of the simplified hand. In the zero-width case, the following group will get the number of the first card. In the one-width case, the group will capture the second card.

The group simply grabs one character, then we must find 3 more copies of that group, but allow any prefix before each repetition. If we promised that the hand was always ordered, the extra stuff before the backreference would not be needed, but it does no harm in being zero width.

Playing Poker (Part 4)

Keeping in mind that we need only minimally identify each type of hand within the corresponding function, not rule out other higher ranked hands, we can take several different approaches to poker regexen.

Recall our possible hands:

- is_four_of_kind(hand)
- is_full_house(hand)
- is_three_of_kind(hand)
- is_two_pairs(hand)
- is_pair()

Four-of-a-kind we did in the last puzzle, so now we want to deal with a full house. Write a function, using regular expressions as much as possible, to identify a hand that contains a full house.

Before you turn the page...

You might risk identifying the "dead man's hand."

One approach you might take for this puzzle is to identify both `is_three_of_kind()` and `is_pair()` in the same hand. Every full house will match those functions. However, in many of the obvious implementations of those support functions, the two initial cards that make up a triple would trigger `is_pair()` even if the last two cards are unmatched. There are ways to make that work, but let's instead do it directly.

For this solution we use regular expressions to strip the suits, and also to match the actual pattern. We can utilize the `cardsort()` function, from Part 1 of the poker puzzles, to guarantee the hand is sorted; we also make sure it is the "pretty" version rather than the ASCII version since sorting assumes that.

The pattern itself is either two of the high number followed by three of the low number, or three of the high number followed by two of the low number. For later use, we can be extra nice by returning the 3-card number first as the "truthy" value in a match. In most poker rules, the 3-card match takes precedence when the same hands are evaluated for the win.

```
>>> def is_full_house(hand):
...     try:
...         hand = prettify(hand)
...     except:
...         pass  # Already pretty
...     hand = cardsort(hand)
...     hand = re.sub(r'[^AKQJT98765432]', '', hand)
...     # Either three of suit then two of other, or
...     # Two of suit then three of other
...     pat = r"^((.)\2{1,2})((.)\4{1,2})$"
...     match = re.search(pat, hand)
...     if not match:
...         return False
...     elif len(match.group(3)) > len(match.group(1)):
...         return hand[4] + hand[0]
...     else:
...         return hand[0] + hand[4]
```

```
>>> is_full_house(prettify('AS AC 8H 8D 8C'))
'8A'
>>> is_full_house(prettify('AS AH AC 8D 8C'))
'A8'
>>> is_full_house(prettify('AS AH JD 8D 8C'))
False
```

Obviously, this solution involves a moderate amount of non-regex Python. But the heart of it is the same reduction to number-only we saw with is_four_of_kind() followed by the pattern described. The just-Python part is really only to provide the friendly truthy values, not in asking the predicate itself.

Figure 15: clown-28772

Playing Poker (Part 5)

In the last few puzzles we identified four-of-a-kind and full house. Much of the logic for this puzzle will be similar to those, but obviously tweaked somewhat for the next cases.

All you have left in our poker regex family is to identify three-of-a-kind, a pair, and two pairs. As before, you may assume that tests for various hands will run in descending order of strength. So, for example, if your test for a pair will incidentally detect a hand that has four-of-a-kind, that is not a problem since it indeed ipso facto has a pair.

Create these three functions in this puzzle:

- is_three_of_kind(hand)
- is_two_pairs(hand)
- is_pair()

Before you turn the page...

Remember that three is more than two, but less than four.

CREATING FUNCTIONS USING REGEXEN

Identifying two- or three-of-a-kind is a lot like identifying four-of-a-kind, just with fewer repetitions. We could do it without sorting the hand, but doing so, as with our full house solution, is a bit easier.

```
>>> def is_three_of_kind(hand):
...     try:
...         hand = prettify(hand)
...     except:
...         pass   # Already pretty
...     hand = cardsort(hand)
...     hand = re.sub(r'[^AKQJT98765432]', '', hand)
...     pat = r'(.)\1{2}'   # No begin/end markers
...     match = re.search(pat, hand)
...     return match.group(1) if match else False
...
...
>>> is_three_of_kind('AS 6H QH 6S 2D')
False
>>> is_three_of_kind('AS 6H QH 6S 6D')
'6'
```

Identifying a pair is basically identical. We simply need to settle for one copy of a card number rather than two copies.

```
def is_pair(hand):
    try:
        hand = prettify(hand)
    except:
        pass   # Already pretty
    hand = cardsort(hand)
    hand = re.sub(r'[^AKQJT98765432]', '', hand)
    pat = r'(.)\1'   # No begin/end markers
    match = re.search(pat, hand)
    return match.group(1) if match else False
```

Matching two pairs is actually a little trickier. Remember that for a full house we matched either two of one number followed by three of the other, or matched the reverse, three then two. However, the "gap" of an unmatched number can occur in more different ways in this case. Thinking about it, two pairs might look like any of the following (even assuming sorting):

PLAYING POKER (PART 5)

- X X _ Y Y
- _ X X Y Y
- X X Y Y _

The unmatched number cannot occur in sorted positions 2 or 4 since that leaves only three cards to the other side of the unmatched number (and we have stipulated sorted order of the hand).

As elsewhere, we return the helpful "truthy" value that might be used later in comparing hands of the same type (namely, the two numbers of the pairs, in sorted order).

```
>>> def is_two_pairs(hand):
...     try:
...         hand = prettify(hand)
...     except:
...         pass  # Already pretty
...     hand = cardsort(hand)
...     hand = re.sub(r'[^[AKQJT98765432]', '', hand)
...     # Three ways to match with unmatched number
...     pat = (r"(.)\1.(.)\2|"
...            r".(.)\3(.)\4|"
...            r"(.)\5(.)\6.")
...     match = re.search(pat, hand)
...     if not match:
...         return False
...     else:
...         return ''.join(n for n in match.groups() if n)
...
>>> is_two_pairs('AH 6S 3H AD 6C')
'A6'
>>> is_two_pairs('AH 6S 3H AD 3C')
'A3'
>>> is_two_pairs('AH 6S 3H KD 3C')
False
```

The remainder of your poker game program is left for a further exercise. The rest of what you'd need to do won't have much to do with regular expressions, simply usual program flow and data structures.

Figure 16: Naive_Scribble_Verso

Easy, Difficult, and Impossible Tasks

Some things are difficult or impossible with regular expressions, and many are elegant and highly expressive. The puzzles in this section ask you to think about which situation each puzzle describes.

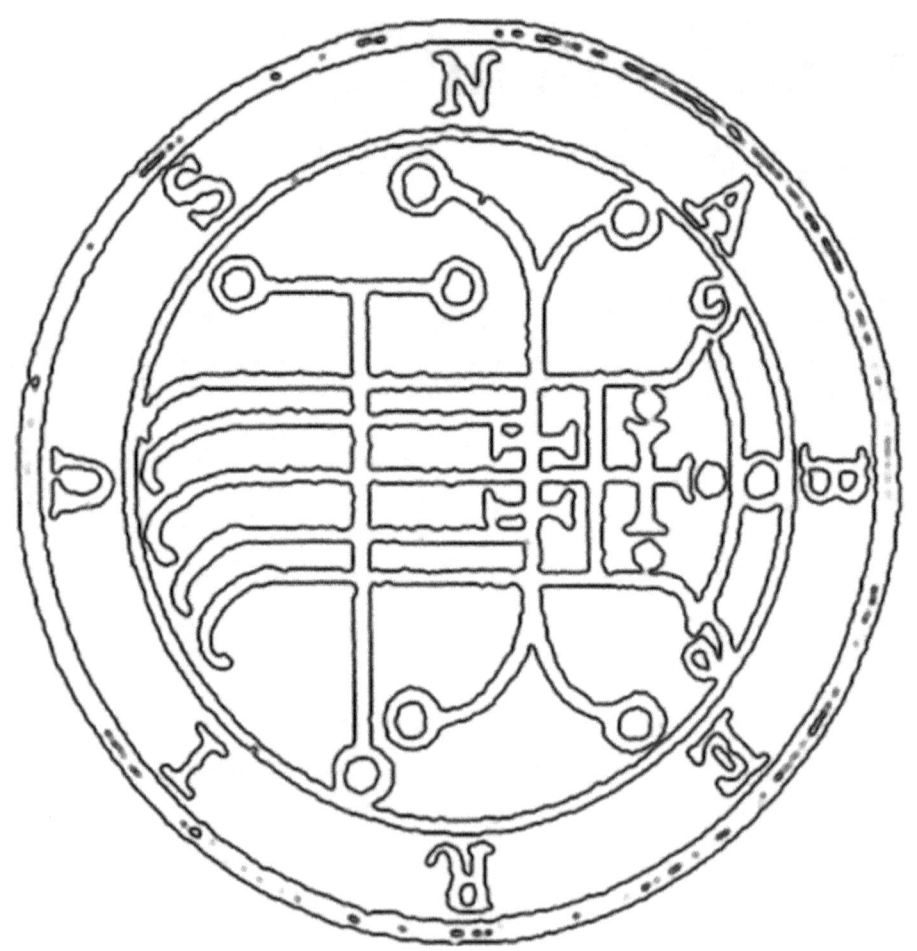

Figure 17: N_A_B_E_R_I_U_S

Identifying Equal Counts

At times we encounter a message or a stream that uses balanced "increment" and "decrement" symbols. For example, one way to check that a message has terminated might be to match up the increments and decrements. The same concept would apply to many kinds of messages and symbols—perhaps you'd like to set the table with the same number of forks and knives, for example.

As a simplification of the general problem, write a regular expression that matches strings that consist of any number of 'A' characters, followed by the same number of 'B' characters.

For example AAABBB and AAAAAAABBBBBBB should match, while AAAABBBBBB should fail to match.

Before you turn the page...

Lateral thinking might help you find the answer.

You cannot match patterns based on having an equal number of different symbols using regular expressions. Or at least you cannot do so in the general case. It is, of course, perfectly possible to require exactly seven 'A's and exactly seven 'B's. But if the count is arbitrarily large, the kind of "machine" that can match the message requires additional power.

In computer science or mathematical terms, a regular expression is equivalet to a *nondeterministic finite automaton* (NFA), where a regex provides a very compact spelling of such an NFA. More powerful machines include *pushdown automata* (PDA) which have an indefinitely large "stack" of stored symbols. One most often encounters PDAs as parsers. A PDA, even the nondeterministic variety, remains formally less powerful than a Turing Machine.

In simple terms, if you want to count occurrences, you need to use variables that can store a number (or a data structure like a list to hold the symbols).

Many new users of regexen fall into a trap of hoping this puzzle is solvable. Or more often still, something equivalent like matching up opening and closing parentheses, brackets, or XML/HTML tags. *Hic sunt dracones*! (Here be dragons)

Matching Before Duplicate Words

If you looked at the last puzzle, you saw that some match patterns you might anticipate to be possible with regular expressions are actually not expressible with regexen. Think about whether this puzzle is possible and, if so, how.

Write a regular expression that will match all the initial words of a string (including any punctuation or spacing that might surround words), stopping before any word that is duplicated in the string. For example:

```
s1 = "this and that not other"
assert re.match(pat, s1).group() == s1
```

Remember that re.match() always starts at the beginning of a string when looking for a match. If you preferred re.search() you would need to begin the pattern with ^. In the first example no word is duplicated in the phrase, and therefore the entire phrase matches. In contrast:

```
s2 = "this and that and other"
assert re.match(pat, s2).group() == 'this '
```

The second example is a little different. The first word 'this' never reoccurs. But the second word 'and' does occur later in the phrase, and therefore it, and everything following the duplicated word, must be excluded.

Before you turn the page...

Find a pattern that will fulfill the requirment.

This match pattern is indeed possible to write as a regular expression. We need to use backreferences to check it, but those are a standard feature of regular expression engines.

```
pat = r'((\w+\b)(?!.*\2\b)\W*)+'
```

As well as the backreference, we use a negative lookahead assertion. That is, the basic thing being matched is (\w+\b)\W*)+. That is to say, match one or more alphanumeric characters \w followed by a word boundary. That "word" might be followed by zero or more non-alphanumeric characters. Then overall, match one or more repetitions of that general pattern.

So far, so good. But we have not excluded the repeated words. We do that with the negative lookahead, (?!.*\2\b). That is, we want to look through the entire rest of the string being evaluated, and make sure that we do not encounter the same word currently matched. The initial .* just matches any number of characters, but the \2 is the actual current word. We still use word boundary in the negative lookahead because a longer word of which the current word is a prefix would be permitted.

Keep in mind how groups are numbered. Since there are parentheses surrounding the entire expression (other than the + quantifier), that whole thing is group 1. So the first subpattern inside of that, matching the current word, is group 2, hence named as \2.

Testing an IPv4 Address

"Internet protocol version 4" addresses are prevalent in almost everything we do with computers. "Under the hood" (so to speak), an IPv4 address is just a 32-bit unsigned integer. However, it is universal to write them in a human-memorable way as so-called dotted quads. In that format, each byte of the address is represented as a decimal number between 0 and 255 (the range of an integer byte), and the four bytes are separated by periods.

Some particular address ranges have special or reserved meanings, but they remain IPv4 addresses, and should be matched for this puzzle. Can you write a regular expression to test if a string is a valid IPv4 address? Some examples:

- Valid: 192.168.20.1
- Invalid: 292.168.10.1
- Invalid: 5.138.0.21.23
- Invalid: 192.AA.20.1

The first of these is a good address; it happens to be a range reserved for internal addresses within an organization (usually one particular router), and hence exists in many local networks. The others fail for various reasons. The first invalid address contains numbers outside the permitted integer range in one quad. The second invalid address has 5 dotted elements rather than 4. The third invalid address contains characters other than decimal digits in one of the quads.

Before you turn the page...

Ask whether regexen are powerful enough for a problem.

It would be very easy to match naive *dotted quads* that simply consisted of four numbers with up to three digits, separated by dots. You might express that as:

`pat = r'^(\d{1-3}){3}\.\d{1-3}$'`

This code will indeed match every IPv4 address. But it will also match many things that are invalid, such as 992.0.100.13. Matching three-digit numbers that begin with 3-9 are definitely wrong. We can try to fix that oversight by allowing only acceptable hundreds digits:

`pat = r'^([12]?\d{1-2}){3}\.[12]?\d{1-2}$'`

This has far fewer false positives. It says "maybe start with a '1' or a '2', then follow that by one or two more digits" (repeating that for dotted quads). So far, so good: 992.0.100.13 is ruled out. But we still might accept 271.10.199.3 which has an invalid first quad.

To fix the pattern we have to *bite the bullet* and list all and only quads we can allow. That is, if a quad starts with a '25' and has three digits, the next digit can only be 0-5. And if it starts with a '2' it definitely cannot have a digit more than 5 next.

```
pat = (
    '^((25[0-5]|2[0-4]\d|[01]?\d\d?)\.){3}'
    '(25[0-5]|2[0-4]\d|[01]?\d\d?)$'
)
```

The pattern is a bit of a mouthful, but when we see how it is built up, the pattern becomes quite clear and elegant. All the stuff after the number quantifier {3} is just a repetition of the earlier subpattern. This is simply because we match three numbers that are followed by a period, but the final number must not be followed by anything.

The main subpattern is just an alternation of options. Maybe the quad looks like 25[0-5]. Or maybe it looks like 2[0-4]\d. These describe all the valid numbers in the 200+ range. For the rest, we get a little clever.

If the quad isn't three digits beginning with a '2', it can either be three-digits beginning with '1' or '0'. Conventionally, leading zeros are dropped, but that is not required. However, two-digit or one-digit numbers are also common; any such two- or one-digit numbers are permitted. So we make the initial [01] optional, and also make the final digit optional with \d?. This gives all and only the remaining permissible quads.

TESTING AN IPV4 ADDRESS

Figure 18: joker-48067975746

Matching a Numeric Sequence

Here's a giveaway for you. This puzzle is *possible* to solve. I won't give you that same assurance when I describe the next two (related) puzzles.

Regular expressions do not really understand numbers. A '7' or a '777' might be sequences of digits matched in a string, but they are not fundamentally different, to regexen, than any other character patterns. Quantifiers can express numbers, either 0/1 with ?, 0 or more with *, or 1 or more with +. In extended regexen like Python uses, we can even express specific counts like {3,6} for "at least three and not more than 6." But those are specific numbers, not calculated quantities.

Nonetheless, we would like to recognize a distinct integer sequence, and rule out other integer sequences, using a regular expression. The trick here is that we can represent an integer as repetitions of the same character, and the number of such repetitions can (to us, at least) represent numbers.

Specifically, for this puzzle, you would like to identify strings that represent successive doublings, and exclude all strings that do not have that pattern. We use the symbol '@' for one unit simply because it is available and doesn't have special meaning with regex patterns. Spaces can separate numbers from each other. So for example:

```
>>> s1 = "@@@ @@@@@@ @@@@@@@@@@@@ "   # 3 6 12
>>> s2 = "@ @@ @@@@ @@@@@@@@ @@@@@@@@@@@@@@@@ "  # 1 2 4 8 16
>>> s3 = "@@ @@@@ @@@@@ @@@@@@@@@@ "  # 2 4 5 10
>>> s4 = "@ @ @@ @@@@ "  # 1 1 2 4
>>> for s in (s1, s2, s3, s4):
...     match = re.search(pat, s)
...     if match:
...         print("VALID", match.group())
...     else:
...         print("INVALID", s)
...
VALID @@@ @@@@@@ @@@@@@@@@@@@
VALID @ @@ @@@@ @@@@@@@@ @@@@@@@@@@@@@@@@
INVALID @@ @@@@ @@@@@ @@@@@@@@@@
INVALID @ @ @@ @@@@
```

MATCHING A NUMERIC SEQUENCE

The pattern you come up with should match strings of any length that follow the doubling sequence, and should reject strings of any length that fail to follow it all the way to their end. The final "number" in a string will always be followed by a space, otherwise it won't have been terminated and shouldn't match.

Before you turn the page...

Be sure to rule out the strings that do not express the sequence.

Let's start with the solution, then explain why it works.

`pat = r"^(((@+) )(?=\3\3 ))+(\3\3 )$"`

What we do here is several steps:

First, make sure we are beginning at the start of the string ('^'). This is where 's4' failed; it doubles as a suffix, but we are required to start at the beginning.

Second, match at least one @ symbol, up to however many occur in a row. After that group of @ symbols, we have a space that is not part of the group.

Third, *lookahead* to a pattern that has twice as many @ symbols as the group we last saw. I spelled that as \3\3, which feels intuitive, but you could likewise spell it as \3{2} to mean the same thing.

Fourth, and finally, after all those repetitions of lookaheads and groups, collect the same pattern as the lookahead just before the end of the string. We want to have the entire sequence in `match.group()`, not to leave off the last "number."

Matching the Fibonacci Sequence

Here we get to something harder than the last puzzle. It is not obvious whether regular expressions are powerful enough to express this sequence. Think about your solution, or the reasons it is impossible, before you turn the page.

The Fibonacci sequence is a famous recursive relationship, in which each number in the sequence is the sum of the prior two numbers. Hence, the first few Fibonacci numbers are:

1 1 2 3 5 8 13 21 34 55 89 144

In fact, the Fibonacci sequence is only one of an infinite number of similar recursive sequences, known generally as Lucas sequences. The Lucas numbers are one such sequence in which the initial elements are 2 and 1 (rather than 1 and 1). We are actually interested here in matching "Fibonacci-like" sequences, where given two elements, the next one is the sum of those prior two.

As in the last puzzle, we represent numeric sequences by a number of repetitions of the @ symbol followed by spaces. For example:

```
# Match: 1 1 2 3 5 8
fibs = "@ @ @@ @@@ @@@@@ @@@@@@@@ "
# Match: 2 1 3 4 7 11
lucas = "@@ @ @@@ @@@@ @@@@@@@ @@@@@@@@@@@ "
# Match: 3 1 4 5 9 14
fib2 = "@@@ @ @@@@ @@@@@ @@@@@@@@@ @@@@@@@@@@@@@@ "
# Fail: 1 1 3 4 7 11
wrong1 = "@ @ @@@ @@@@ @@@@@@@ @@@@@@@@@@@ "
# Fail: 1 1 2 3 4 7
wrong2 = "@ @ @@ @@@ @@@@ @@@@@@@ "
```

Can you create a regular expression that matches only Fibonacci-like sequences within encoded strings?

Before you turn the page...

The Golden Spiral beautifully generalizes Fibonacci Numbers.

It turns out that matching properly encoded Fibonacci-like sequences is within the power of regular expressions. Adding together two prior elements is actually a lot like simply doubling the one prior element as we did in the last puzzle.

The main difference in the solution to this puzzle versus the last one is that we need to backreference two groups in the lookahead pattern rather than just one. Study the explanation of the last puzzle before looking at the solution to this one.

```
>>> pat1 = r"^(((@+) (@+) )(?=$|\3\4 ))+(\3\4)?$"
>>> pat2 = r"^@+ (((@+) (@+) )(?=\3\4 ))+"
>>> for s in (fibs, lucas, fib2, wrong1, wrong2):
...     match = re.search(pat1, s)
...     if match and re.search(pat2, s):
...         print("VALID", match.group())
...     else:
...         print("INVALID", s)
...
VALID @ @ @@ @@@ @@@@@ @@@@@@@@
VALID @@ @ @@@ @@@@ @@@@@@@ @@@@@@@@@@@
VALID @@@ @ @@@@ @@@@@ @@@@@@@@@ @@@@@@@@@@@@@@
INVALID @ @ @@@ @@@@ @@@@@@@ @@@@@@@@@@
INVALID @ @ @@ @@@ @@@@ @@@@@@@
```

Actually, there are two extra caveats here. We assume in this solution that an even number of numbers are represented in the string. The lookahead only evaluates the one next number (that must be the sum of the current two numbers). However, this means that we match two different '@' sequences at a time; and hence that there must be an even number if we match to the end.

The second issue is that since we stride two-by-two through the "numbers," we need to use a second regular expression to make sure the sequence *predicts* the next element when offset by one element as well. We see that problem in wrong1. If we only utilized pat1 it would incorrectly match as Fibonacci-like. Since pat1 already collects the final "number," there is no need for pat2 to do so as well; the lookahead suffices.

Figure 19: Naive_Scribble_Recto

Matching the Prime Numbers

Perhaps surprisingly, in the last puzzle we were able to match Fibonacci-like sequences using regular expressions. Let's turn next to whether we might do the same thing with prime numbers. In particular, if you can find it, your regular expression(s) will only need to match ascending initial sequences of the primes, but all such initial sequences.

As in the last two puzzles, we encode numeric sequences using a number of contiguous @ symbols, with each "number" separated by spaces. For example:

```
# Match: 2 3 5 7
primes4 = "@@ @@@ @@@@@ @@@@@@@ "
# Match: 2 3 5 7 11
primes5 = "@@ @@@ @@@@@ @@@@@@@ @@@@@@@@@@@ "
# Fail: 2 3 7 11
fail1 = "@@ @@@ @@@@@@@ @@@@@@@@@@@ "
# Fail: 2 3 4 5 7
fail2 = "@@ @@@ @@@@ @@@@@ @@@@@@@ "
```

The Sieve of Eratosthenes is a lovely and ancient algorithm for finding all the prime numbers. It "strikes out" each multiple of a prime as it steps through all the natural numbers, leaving only primes thereby. In a compact Python implementation it can look like the below (this can be made much more efficient, but at the price of more code).

```
def get_primes():
    "Simple lazy Sieve of Eratosthenes"
    candidate = 2
    found = []
    while True:
        if all(candidate % prime != 0 for prime in found):
            yield candidate
            found.append(candidate)
        candidate += 1
```

MATCHING THE PRIME NUMBERS

The form of the Sieve is definitely reminiscent of lookahead assertions which we have used in many of the puzzles. Think about whether you can implement this using regular expressions (don't think about performance for this puzzle). Before you look at the discussion, try either to find a regular expression to match the valid sequences or to formulate clearly why you cannot.

Before you turn the page...

Honor the Fundamental Theorem of Arithmetic.

This puzzle turns out to be another one that exceeds the ability of regular expressions. On the face of it, it might seem like *negative lookahead assertions* are exactly what you would use to implement the Sieve, or something akin to it. That is, if some group matched, e.g. (@@@) or (@+), then you should be able to backreference to a repetition of that group.

Let's say the hypothetical group was number 7. In that case, a negative lookahead assertion like (?! \7{2,}) would state precisely that no contiguous numbers of @ symbols, whose count is a multiple of the number in the prior match group, occur later in the string. That sounds a lot like what the Sieve does.

Negative lookahead is indeed a powerful and useful technique. In fact, you could perfectly well implement a partial sieve to exclude all the multiples of the first N primes from occurring in a candidate string. The problem is that regular expressions can only have a finite number of match groups by definition. That is, regular expressions are a way of expressing *finite state* machines. The exact maximum number of groups can vary between regex engines; it is 100 in the Python standard library re module, 500 in the third-party regex module, and various other numbers in other programming languages or libraries. But it is always a finite number.

To match *every* string of initial primes, we need to "strike out" indefinitely many primes along the way. This same problem would occur for every other sequential prime-finding algorithm. There do exist direct primality tests that do not iterate through the smaller primes, such as the probabilistic Miller–Rabin test[2] or the deterministic Agrawal–Kayal–Saxena test. However, all of those require mathematical calculations that are not possible in regular expressions.

---

[2]A version of the Miller-Rabin test can be made deterministic if the Generalized Riemann hypothesis holds.

Figure 20: Olives_Recto

Matching Relative Prime Numbers

If you read the last puzzle, you saw the subtle reason why a regular expression cannot match an initial sequence of primes. Think *finite automaton*. If you skipped that puzzle, at least go back and refresh your understanding of the Sieve of Eratosthenes.

Mathematics has a concept of *relative primes* which is slightly weaker than primality. All prime numbers are relatively prime—also called *coprime*—with each other, but other pairs are as well. Two coprime numbers have no common divisors other than 1. This is certainly true of prime numbers; for example, 11 and 53 are relatively prime since neither have any divisors other than themselves and 1. But likewise 10 and 21 are coprime since the divisors of the first are 2 and 5, but those of the second are 3 and 7, which do not overlap.

So the question for this puzzle is whether you can create an expression that will identify all and only sequences of ascending natural numbers where all of them are relatively prime to each other. Trivially, any sequence of ascending primes qualifies here, but so do other sequences.

As in the last three puzzles, we encode numeric sequences using a number of contiguous @ symbols, with each "number" separated by spaces. For example:

MATCHING RELATIVE PRIME NUMBERS

```
# Match: 2 3 5 7 11
primes5 = "@@ @@@ @@@@@ @@@@@@@ @@@@@@@@@@@ "
# Match: 2 5 7 9 11
relprime1 = "@@ @@@@@ @@@@@@@ @@@@@@@@@ @@@@@@@@@@@ "
# Match: 3 4 7 11
relprime2 = "@@@ @@@@ @@@@@@@ @@@@@@@@@@@ "
# Match: 9 16
startbig = "@@@@@@@@@ @@@@@@@@@@@@@@@@ "
# Fail: 2 3 4 5 7  (2, 4 relatively composite)
fail1 = "@@ @@@ @@@@ @@@@@ @@@@@@@ "
# Fail: 5 7 2 3 11 (all primes, non-ascending)
fail2 = "@@@@@ @@@@@@@ @@ @@@ @@@@@@@@@@@ "
```

Are relative primes consigned to the same fate as primes?

Before you turn the page...

Nothing is either true or false but thinking makes it so.

There are a couple of issues to consider in this solution. It turns out that such a solution is indeed possible, using much the same style as the Sieve of Eratosthenes, but not an identical technique. That is, as discussed in the last puzzle, we are perfectly well able to reject a string based on a future multiple of a given number.

The trick is that we do not need to reject *infinitely* many if we do not assume that a string needs to contain all the initial primes. Instead, we can focus just on a single number at a time, and rule out *its* multiples. We might miss some primes in our sequence, or indeed have some relatively prime composite numbers. But that satisfies the current puzzle.

However, for this "striking through" to work, we need also to enforce the rule that sequences are ascending. Otherwise, we might encounter, e.g. @@@@@@@@ @@@@ @@ (i.e. '8 4 2'). Those are definitely not mutually coprime. However, "stricking out" multiples of 8 does not help reject 4 later in the string. Python only allows fixed length lookbehind assertions, but some other regex implementation could technically relax this ascending sequence restriction (however, a library that did so would quickly face catastrophic exponential complexity in this case).

```
pat = r'^((@@+) (?=\2@)(?!.* \2{2,} ))+'
```

Here we first identify a group of 2 or more @ symbols. Then we do a postive lookahead to ensure that the next group of @ symbols has at least one more symbol.

The real crux of this is the *negative lookahead* assertion that we never later see a (space delimited) sequence of two or more copies of the group. This pattern does not capture the final "number" in the sequence; it is just used to provide a true or false answer to whether the sequence matches.

www.ingramcontent.com/pod-product-compliance
Lightning Source LLC
Chambersburg PA
CBHW072227170526
45158CB00002BA/793